QUANTUM WRITING

How to Write Like a Pro

by

Bobbi DePorter
with Mike Hernacki

Learning Forum Publications
Oceanside, California USA

Dedicated to all the very special Learning Forum staff
who over the years have contributed so much.
I acknowledge Vicki Gibbs for her contribution in the writing of
Write Like a Pro

LEARNING FORUM PUBLICATIONS
1725 South Coast Highway
Oceanside, CA 92054-5319 USA
(760) 722-0072
(760) 722-3507 fax
email: info@learningforum.com
www.learningforum.com

Cover design by Kelley Thomas
Illustrations by Ellen Duris

ISBN: 0-945525-27-3

Write Like a Pro

? *Is there a way to make the writing process easier?*

? *Can you learn to write creatively even if you don't consider yourself creative?*

? *You're a very good speaker, yet you don't feel as comfortable with your writing. What can you do?*

? *You're unsure of your spelling, and suspect it affects your writing. Is there anything you can do about it?*

Contents

1

You're a Natural

We're all writers at heart. As young children, we were truly uninhibited writers, eager to express ourselves using vivid, creative thoughts and language. As we grew older, though, we became critical of our writing and began to dread having to do anything that involves putting words on paper.

For many people, writing has been a painful process, one they delay as long as possible. When they're finally forced to put something on paper, they end up sending out a hurried draft that doesn't say what they meant and is often filled with careless mistakes. It doesn't have to be that way. You can learn to take the pain out of writing.

What we need now is to get back in touch with that child in us who was eager to write down thoughts and ideas. And the way to do that is to not worry about the finished product when we're just starting the process.

When you bake a cake, do you worry about how it's going to look sitting on the serving platter? No, you just start breaking eggs. When you undertake to fix your car, are you concerned about how it will look going down the street after the repair? No, you put your attention on finding the problem and taking off the malfunctioning part. Then why fret about your final draft as soon as you sit down to write?

Logic and our own experience tell us to begin by dealing with the problems of getting started. Writing is actually a process; it isn't about throwing the throttle forward and taking off. In order to write the way we want to write, we have to plan and prepare.

Writing also requires practice. Like running, the more we do it the better we get at it. Some days we don't want to run and we resist every step of the way but we do it anyway. We practice whether we want to or not. We don't wait around for inspiration and a deep desire to run. It'll never happen, especially if we are out of shape and

We're all natural writers at heart.

Stop worrying about the finished product — just start writing!

have been avoiding it. But if we run regularly, we train our mind to cut through or ignore the resistance. We just do it. And suddenly in the middle of the run, we love it. That's how writing is too. Once we are deep into it, we wonder what took us so long to finally settle down at the desk. Through practice we actually get better. We learn to trust ourselves and our writing more.

The best way NOT to write, is to sit down and say, "I'm going to write a brilliant poem now." That attitude will freeze us right away because even saying brilliant implies judgment. Sit down instead without any expectations – turn off your inner critic and give yourself the space to write without any predetermined destination.

If you decide to write the great American novel, it will be difficult to write that first sentence. If every time we sit down to write, we expect something great, writing will be a disappointment.

Even professional writers have anxious moments when facing a blank page or screen. To get past that initial panic, break the writing process down into three different steps:

1. Plan It
2. Write It
3. Polish It

To get past initial "Writer's Block," break the writing process down into three different steps.

Follow these steps:

1   Plan It (Prewriting)
Organize thoughts and ideas

2   Write It
Keep it clear, concise, and simple

3   Polish It
Edit final product

2

Plan It

For most people, the hardest part of writing is getting the first few words on paper. Many of us refer to this as "writer's block." In reality, it's more like "writer's pause," and novice writers get stuck at this stage because they fail to carefully plan what they're going to write. They just sit down at their desk or turn on their computer totally unprepared—and then expect the words to flow. It doesn't work that way. Before you even think about sentence length and which paragraph goes where, you've got to decide just what points your writing will include. You've got to get the ideas flowing. That's where the Plan It (also called the "prewriting") stage of the process comes in.

Prewriting is probably the most important—and most overlooked—phase of writing. Used correctly, it helps you develop thoughts, break past "writer's pause," and organize your ideas. The prewriting techniques below are dramatically different from the traditional outlining techniques you probably learned in school—and with good reason. Outlining is a left-brain function, logical and analytical. Developing outlines helps you to organize your ideas, and can be useful . . . once you've come up with those ideas. Prewriting, on the other hand, taps into the right side of your brain, the more creative side. It helps you come up with the ideas in the first place by letting your thoughts emerge in a random, free-flowing fashion. This allows you to explore a much wider range of ideas than the traditional outlining approach does.

There are two basic techniques that make up the planning/prewriting stage:

- Brainstorming and
- Mind Mapping®

Prewriting helps you generate and explore ideas.

These techniques make up this stage:

Brainstorming

::

Mind Mapping®

How extensively you plan depends on what you have to write. For a short, simple memo, you might simply jot down the ideas you want to cover and then number them in the order you want them to go. If you're struggling with a longer, more complex and detailed piece of writing, you may want to use all of the techniques described below.

Don't feel compelled to use all of these techniques each time you write, though. They're simply tools to help you unblock your mind, tap into your imagination, and put your ideas down on paper. Use the technique that works best for you and fits your learning style.

Brainstorming

Think about the power in a storm: the lightning flashing, the wind howling, the rain driving down. Then let loose some similar energy in your brain. Free-associate ideas in a random, unstructured form. Don't censor your thoughts; simply write them down as quickly as you can. Let them flow without any control.

Before you start, though, take a minute to ask yourself:
- Who is my audience?
- What is the purpose of this writing?
- What tone do I want to project?
- What goal do I hope to achieve with what I write?

For example, maybe you need to send a letter to a customer whose payment is overdue. He's a good person and you don't want to alienate him, but you do want your money. In this case:
- Your audience is obviously the customer.
- The purpose of your letter would be to remind him, in a non-threatening manner, that he owes you money.
- Your tone needs to be firm but pleasant. Keep it positive, but make it clear he does owe you the money.

Before you start,
take a minute
to ask yourself:

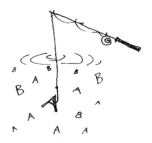

- Who is my audience?
- What is the purpose of this writing?
- What tone do I want to project?
- What goal do I hope to achieve with what I write?

- As for the goal, you hope he'll whip out his checkbook and pay your bill immediately.

One way to begin your brainstorm is by clustering. Developed by Gabriele Rico, this brainstorming technique is used by many professional writers to get ideas flowing.

At first glance, a cluster looks a lot like a Mind Map. Although both can be used for brainstorming, a cluster is less structured, more free-flowing, allowing for quick associations. We'll use Mind Maps later in the writing process. With clustering, you just let your mind go. You approach the piece you're writing holistically; that is, you look at the big picture and the let the details come later. It's almost like "free-associating" on paper.

Clusters serve as a visual representation of the way your mind sorts information. Starting with a central thought in the middle of the page, you branch your ideas off from the core idea, ultimately building a many-spoked structure with a multitude of ideas. Just write your ideas around the central thought, circle them, and then draw lines connecting them either to the central thought or to a related idea. Your cluster will look like a model of a molecule.

The whole purpose is to let your thoughts flow freely. Here are some suggestions to get you started:
- Take a key word or phrase about your subject and write it in the middle of your paper. Then draw a circle around it.
- Now jot down all the associations you can make, clustering them around your central thought. Draw a circle around each word as you write it and draw a line to the central thought.
- Write down any secondary ideas that were sparked by these words and again circle them, this time

Clustering is a brainstorming technique — it gets the ideas flowing.

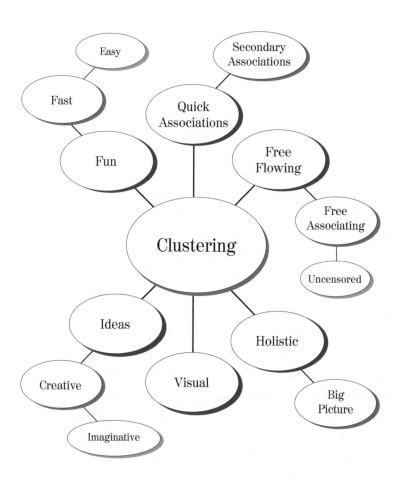

A cluster on "clustering."

drawing a line to the word that sparked the idea.
And on and on.
- Allow the spokes and circles to be free-flowing; you'll organize them later.

The right page shows a cluster of the letter to the overdue customer. The next step is to go through the ideas and cross out any you don't want to use. In this cluster, you might cross out "has 2 children" and "need money," since you probably wouldn't want to include that in your letter.

Then, star your main points: reminder notice, due dates, good customer. These are the points you will focus on in your letter. Finally, put all the ideas (except those you crossed out) in sequential order. Number them in the order you would like them to appear in your letter. (Don't worry if the order changes somewhat when you write your letter.)

You don't have to use every thought that comes to you when you brainstorm and you certainly don't have to write them in the order you came up with them. Just use the ideas as a base and go from there.

When brainstorming, lose the editor. When most people write, they can hear two competing voices in their heads at the same time. The first voice is the writer: creative, free-flowing, imaginative, and uncensored . . . perfect for brain-storming. The other is the editor, a jarring voice that jumps in when they've barely begun to write and points out each little repetition or error in grammar and structure. While this voice can be helpful later on in the writing process, it can be deadly in the early stages. It's this voice that leads to "writer's pause." So ignore it for now. Do whatever you have to do to quiet it down, and forge ahead.

Clustering is an effective way to generate ideas for a letter.

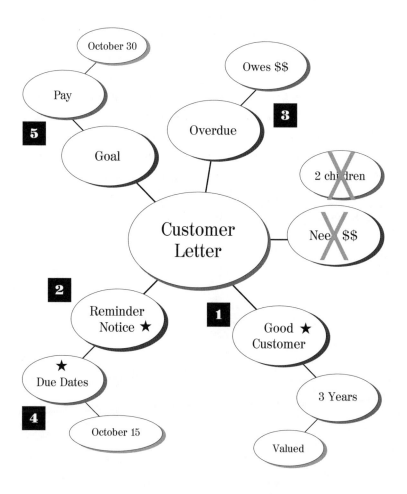

Mind Mapping/Organizing

Once you get your ideas down you can begin developing and organizing your thoughts. This is where your can put your Mind Mapping skills to use.

To Mind Map, take a look at the model on the right-hand page. Notice how it starts with a central idea and branches out to include subtopics and details. Mind Map the numbered points on your cluster and further explore the areas you starred. This organizes your paper and provides you even more ideas to write about.

Mind Mapping the numbered points on the cluster gives you the specifics on how you'll approach John Smith. Your Mind Map might include subpoints or even key phrases, such as including your phone number in the letter, thanking John for something, extending his time to pay without penalty, and clearly stating a date when an additional late fee would be charged. Once you're satisfied with the results, its time to move on to writing it.

Mind Mapping® is useful in developing and organizing your thoughts.

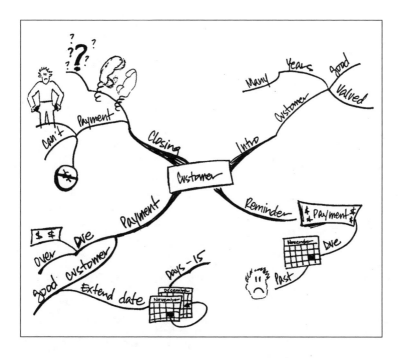

A Mind Map on creating a customer letter.

3

Write It

Freewriting

This is a great technique for lubricating the gears of your writing machine and getting the words flowing. Here's how it works. Pick up your pen, or get on your computer and start writing. Don't make changes or corrections, and definitely don't start over. Forget the rules of punctuation, grammar, and spelling. Just write whatever comes to mind as quickly as you can. Don't worry if your thoughts wander or even stop for a while. Just go with the flow, keep writing, and don't stop until you've completely run out of ideas. To get started, you might want to use the branches of your Mind Map to begin your sentences. Here's an example of freewriting for a letter of reference.

We, small biz. I was looking for a new office for my small biz. Needed more space. Wanted to invest in a small building. My partner and I met with Jill Hall. She found us an office perfect for us, couldn't be happier. Whole thing was good experience. We'd gladly recommend her again to anyone. Very happy. She was professional, affective, friendly, easy to work with. She spent time, showed us numerous office sights. Listened to what we wanted, went out & found it.

Now read the finished letter:

> To Whom It May Concern:
>
> My partner and I recently worked with Jill Hall to purchase a new office building for our small, but growing, business. We couldn't have been more pleased with the work she did for us. She was helpful, friendly, cooperative, professional, and very patient.
>
> Jill willingly showed us a wide variety of buildings in several locations around the city. By work-

When freewriting, forget the rules of grammar and spelling. Go with the flow — write whatever comes to mind.

66 *Start at the beginning, and when you get to the end, stop.* 99

– Lewis Carroll
  Author, Alice in Wonderland

ing with us closely and listening to what we liked and disliked about each building and location, she was able to finally find the perfect property for us.

We love our new office building and Jill made the whole experience a pleasure. She was great to work with and we would gladly recommend her to anyone who is interested in purchasing commercial property.

Sincerely,

Notice the final letter used much of the information from the freewriting version, but did so in an organized, easy-to-read format, with the errors and abbreviations edited out. Once you've completed a freewrite version, you have something concrete to work with, so organizing your thoughts is an easier task. What's left is simply a matter of revising and polishing the final draft. (Note: In practice you would not produce the final draft yet. That comes in the Write It step. We put the finished letter here for illustration purposes.)

Some people use the traditional outline style to organize their freewriting ideas into a final draft. That may work fine for you, but don't get so wrapped up in the format (I, A, 1, a) that you forget about the message. A better method might be the inverted pyramid approach. The idea here is to put the most important information or idea right up front. In other words, start with your conclusion, then back it up.

This method works great for short writings, as well as for some longer pieces. Many writers lose their readers by dragging them along on page after page of introductory or explanatory material before getting to the point. With this technique, rewriting or reorganizing is often just a matter of rearranging the information you have written down. Try doing this: Circle your main idea, then make sure you put it toward the beginning of the doccument.

Organize your freewriting into an inverted pyramid.

**Most Important
Information**
Main Point
Summary
Answers
Requests
Conclusions

**Least Important
Information**
Detail
Explanation
Reasons
Discussions

To reinforce this idea, go back and re-read something you wrote in the past. Could you strengthen the piece by moving the last or next-to-last paragraph and making it the lead paragraph?

You can help your reader by putting the most important information first:

- summary before detail
- answers before explanations
- requests before reasons, and
- conclusions before discussions.

Notice that even though you've done some writing so far, we're just now coming to the actual writing part. The planning and freewriting steps are still preliminary. But you've gotten a lot done. Your main points are complete and organized. You warmed up and you're ready to write!

What you just finished is the hard part. Let this be the fun part.

Natural-Sounding Writing

Someone, somewhere started a rumor that writing and speaking are two completely separate skills...and people seem to accept this as fact. How many times have you heard a person say, "I know what I want to say, and I can tell you easily. But when it comes to putting it down on paper, I just can't." Maybe you've said that yourself.

Guess what: It's not really true, or at least it doesn't have to be. The more we learn about communication, the more obvious it becomes that speaking and writing are in fact closely linked. People who are good at one of them are often also good at the other. Yet skilled speakers or interesting conversationalists often believe they can't write. But that's just a belief. As the song says, it ain't necessarily so.

Speaking and writing skills are closely linked. Most good speakers are also good writers.

Follow these suggestions:

Adopt a natural tone

∷

Try speaking into a tape recorder, then write

∷

Avoid stilted phrases and jargon

Writing consultants use a number of techniques to help people who struggle with writing. One technique is to have those people speak their ideas into a tape recorder and then write from the tape. Try it. You'll be surprised at how it frees you from the tyranny of perfect punctuation and flawless grammar, fear of which can lead to "writer's pause."

Good writing is clear, concise, and sounds natural. You'd probably never deliver a report in-person and say, "Enclosed please find the report which we discussed yesterday, March 25." Why do that in your writing? It's much simpler and clearer to say, "Here's the report we talked about yesterday."

Much of the formal wording we use in communication today is nothing more than a carry-over from the days when people spoke as well as wrote more formally. We learned from writing textbooks that were copied from earlier textbooks that were in turn copied from even earlier textbooks. Today we don't talk like people did in 1890. Why should we write like that?

Another common goal shared by speakers and writers is a desire to effectively reach their target audience. To do it, writers and speakers alike must first decide just who their audience is. Then they must determine just what it is they want to leave their audience (readers) with and what outcome they're striving for themselves. In the case of a memo, for example, the writer may be requesting a new tool or piece of equipment. If so, that needs to be clearly stated in the memo, not left for the readers to figure out unaided.

In addition to sounding natural and knowing your audience, here are some other tips to bear in mind as you write:

Effectively reaching their target audience is a common goal shared by both speakers and writers.

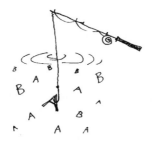

When writing or speaking, ask yourself:

Who's my audience?

::

What is my desired outcome?

::

What do I want to leave them with?

Keep Your Writing Clear, Concise, and Simple

To do this, try to keep your sentences under 20 words. To add interest to your writing, vary the length of your sentences. Choose short words over long words, or as Mark Twain so eloquently expressed it: "I never use 'metropolis' for seven cents a word because I can get the same price for 'city.'" Also keep your paragraphs short and to the point. A good range is four to eight sentences per paragraph.

You can help keep your writing clean and concise by omitting needless words. Eliminate useless "wind-up" words and phrases, which people often stick on the beginning of their sentences and paragraphs.

Examples:

- Per your request, I've asked John to join us at the next gathering.
- As we discussed on the phone, I will order the supplies immediately.

Check the beginning of your sentences to make sure that the first words contain the most important information. If you need to document past correspondence or conversations, put a reference line at the top of your document. You can also include attachments of previous, repetitive facts, figures, and documentation if necessary.

Cutting out excess prepositional phrases, such as *in the future, for the record, of the opinion,* will also strengthen your writing. Stay away from sentences like this:

The goal of the meeting in the morning over in room 342, is to decide, after a brief discussion, the name of the person who will chair next year's committee.

Eliminate all those prepositions and you'll have a clearer sentence . . . one your reader might even understand.

Keep your writing
clear, concise, and simple.

Follow these three guidelines:

Eliminate "wind up" words
and phrases

∷

Put the most important
information first

∷

Eliminate prepositional
phrases whenever possible

At tomorrow morning's brief meeting in room 342 we'll decide who will chair next year's budget committee.

Be Specific

Whenever possible, write about people rather than abstractions. If you know the name of the person, say so in your letter. Don't say "they" if you mean Jon, Sue, and Harold.

Instead of writing:

I sent your article to the editor of that health magazine.

Write:

I sent your article to Judy Cassidy, the editor of Longevity Magazine.

Also, get rid of vague qualifiers. Not only do they rob your writing of impact, they also leave the reader wondering just exactly what you mean. For example, a "small fortune" to you may be two months' salary to your reader. So try to avoid words and phrases like:

- generally
- to some degree
- a number of

Instead of writing, "I'll contact you next week," say "I'll phone you on Tuesday." Rather than vaguely suggesting there will be "several" people attending a meeting, find out how many will be there and put in the correct number.

Use Strong, Active Verbs

Strong verbs give your writing impact. The verb serves as the central word in any sentence: the action, the part of speech that creates movement. Use active verbs to bring your writing to life. Most people rely on weak, inactive verbs . . . probably because they don't know any better. Consequently, their words just "sit" on the page, rather

Precise writing gets greater results.

Give clear directions, exact dates, and deadlines:

"I need it by 2:00 p.m." instead of
"I need it ASAP"

::

"Call us today," instead of
"We'd love to hear from you"

than "pulling" the reader along to the end.

Change your weak verbs to strong ones by limiting the use of all forms of the verb to be. When possible replace i*s, am, are, was, were, will be, can,* and *should be.* Some publishers actually state in their editor's guidelines that every single form of to be should be changed to an active verb. You don't have to go that far, but do use active verbs as much as possible; you'll be surprised at the difference this will make in your writing.

Compare, "Senator Johnson was head of the task force," with, "Senator Johnson headed the task force." See the difference? Rather than, "I am sure you understand our position," try, "I trust you understand our position."

Use the Active Voice

In addition to using active verbs, always try to use the active rather than the passive voice. It keeps your writing lively and interesting. Think of the passive people you know. They let things happen to them. Active people, on the other hand, make things happen. Their lives move. The same is true in writing. Passive voice verbs delay the action; active voice verbs take charge and do the action.

Remember Ronald Reagan's famous comment when he was forced to admit of wrongdoing in his Administration while he was President of the U.S.? He said, "Mistakes were made." By use of the passive voice, he shifted attention onto the "mistakes" and away from the people who made them—but what everyone wanted to know was who did those things! Passive voice is the refuge of the person who doesn't want to communicate clearly as well as the one who doesn't know how.

How can you tell the difference between the passive and the active voice? Think of the actors in the sentences you write. Is the actor doing the action or is the action being

Here's a list of action verbs to keep in mind when you write:

act
adapt
address
analyze
apply
assist

budget
build

calculate
communicate
compile
compute
consult
coordinate

define
determine
devise
distribute
draft

edit
electrify
eliminate
enlarge

familiarize
figure
formulate

gather
govern
guide

head
help
hire

identify
instruct
invent

judge

lead
lecture

manage
mediate
motivate

navigate
negotiate

observe
obtain
organize

participate
persuade
predict
promote

quote

reason
recommend
research
resolve
retrieve
review

save
simplify
solve
specify
stimulate
strengthen
systematize
study

talk
transfer
translate
treat
tutor

unify
upgrade
update

vitalize

write

done? Look at this example of a passive voice sentence:

The meeting agenda for the task force was set by the chairman.

Who's supposed to be the actor in that sentence? The chairman is. But because the writer used the passive voice, the chairman got pushed into the background. To change this sentence from passive to active, ask yourself, "Who does what to whom?" Then switch the words around so that the actor, the subject of the sentence, actually does the action.

The chairman set the meeting agenda for the task force.

By switching this sentence to the active voice you accomplish three things:

- You shift the sentence from passive to active, putting the action back where it belongs . . . with the actor.

- You eliminate the weak "be" verb and substitute the strong, active verb "set."

- You tighten and shorten your sentence, since the proper arrangement of an active-verb sentence is: subject, verb, object. Consequently, the person responsible for the action comes first, not last.

Here's another example of how to change a passive voice sentence into an active voice sentence:

It was decided by the principal to make a formal complaint.

Doesn't the following revised sentence sound clearer and more direct?

The principal decided to make a formal complaint.

Check to see if you're using the passive voice in your writing. Do you frequently find the word "by" followed by what should be the subject of your sentence?

Make your passive sentences active.

Follow these suggestions:

Ask yourself, "Who does what to whom?"

::

Put action with the actor

::

Use this sentence order: Subject, verb, object

Passive – The report was requested by the professor.

Active   – The professor requested the report.

Passive – The report was mailed by his assistant.

Active   – His assistant mailed the report.

Don't Use Clichés or Jargon

Clichés muddy your writing. Although most of us are guilty of using trite expressions in our speech, when we use them extensively in our letters and memos we tag ourselves as lazy writers. Plus, clichés can be misunderstood. So rather than grabbing the first tired, overused expression you can think of, use your own words.

Instead of writing:
   Let's run the idea up the flagpole and see
   if anyone salutes.

Try:
   Let's run the idea past some of our key people and
   see if anyone likes it.

Instead of:
   The news came at me like a bolt from the blue.

Try:
   The news hit me like lightning.

Notice that in my revisions, I did use familiar expressions, such as "run the idea" and "key people." While these are heavily used, they aren't truly the kind of clichés that make people groan. To write originally and creatively, you don't have to take the time to say everything in an entirely new way. It's OK to use familiar expressions because often they have a distinct meaning to your readers. But you must tread the fine line that separates the familiar from the

Avoid clichés and jargon, they confuse the reader and muddy your writing. Say exactly what you mean.

66 *The difference between the right word and the almost right word is the difference between lightning and the lightning bug.* 99

– Mark Twain

banal. While you're doing that, it's easy to get caught in another verbal trap: jargon.

When you've studied or worked in an area for several years, it's easy to fall into the trap of using buzz words, or jargon, that others in your area understand. But when you use those same buzz words and phrases in your writing, you run the risk of being misunderstood, and some readers might even find you pompous. So avoid using acronyms and jargon in your letters and memos unless you're absolutely sure your correspondent will understand them. Unless everyone who will read your letter knows that PAC stands for Political Action Committee, don't use the acronym; spell it out instead and explain it if necessary.

Other phrases to avoid include:
- In the ballpark
- Sad state of affairs
- Enclosed please find

You can probably think of a dozen more. If you've seen an expression more than twice in other people's writing, don't use it.

Use a Respectful Tone

Two of the most appropriate and powerful tones in writing are sincerity and respect. Although humor and sarcasm may work in person, they don't ring true when written. They can easily be misinterpreted and can cause bad feelings. Whether you're writing a long letter or a short E-mail message, never patronize or criticize.

Instead of a patronizing:

I realize you're a very busy person with lots of important meetings to attend but I really, really

In writing,
use a respectful tone.

People

respond

best to

sincerity

and respect.

hope you'll take time from your busy schedule to join us at the meeting next Tuesday.

Try:

I know you have a busy schedule, so this meeting will be brief. I hope you'll be able to attend.

People recognize and appreciate sincerity and respect, and they respond by returning the same to you.

4

Polish It

For many writers, this stage is the best. They've overcome writer's pause, and written everything down in an organized fashion. Now it's time to polish it. Keep the following guidelines in mind as you refine your words and soon your writing will shine like a pro's.

When you edit, ask yourself:
- Did I write for the audience I want to address?
- Is my tone appropriate for my readers?
- Have I used appropriate language? Is my writing natural and comfortable? How would I speak these same paragraphs?
- Have I used strong, active verbs?

Now it's time to proofread your work. Here are some guidelines:

Let It Sit

If you have the time, always wait for a while after writing something before you proofread it—a couple of hours for short pieces, even a few days for longer ones. This allows your ego time to separate from the text so you can evaluate it objectively. You'll also be less likely to read what you believe you wrote, rather than what you *really* wrote.

Read It Aloud

Even if what you've written is for the printed page only, read it out loud. You'll be surprised how this can help you catch mistakes, spelling errors, and wording that just doesn't "sound" right to the reader's internal ear.

Exchange It With a Friend

Be sure it's someone you trust and respect. Ask for feedback, and value what he or she tells you.

"Polish it" — the editing and proofreading stage.

General proofreading guidelines:

Let it sit

::

Read it aloud

::

Get feedback from a friend

::

Read it backwards

::

Use reference materials

::

Take advantage of technology:
spell-checkers, grammar checkers on
word processors

Read It Backwards, from Bottom to Top

This works great for short correspondence. The mistakes really jump out at you because you're reading word-for-word rather than for content.

Use Reference Materials

Learn how to get value from dictionaries, usage handbooks, and style guides. Even the most competent writers rely on outside sources to check spelling and punctuation rules when they need to. And be sure to keep your references up-to-date; styles change, usage changes.

Take Advantage of Modern Technology

Remember not to worry about the grammar, spelling and punctuation until after you've finished your Write It step. But when you do check it, make use of software programs that have spelling and grammar checkers. These can be invaluable tools for any writer. Be sure not to rely totally on these programs, however. Most spelling checkers don't tell you whether or not you've used the right homonym (i.e. their or there, your and you're).

One Last Tip

Always confirm the spelling of individual and company names; those are the misspellings that make the worst impressions. A quick phone call is usually all it takes to insure accuracy and avoid major embarrassment. A man I know lost the chance for some important business when he assumed a prospect's name was "Francis" (male) when actually it was "Frances" (female). It turned out the prospect was sensitive to this mistake and turned down his proposal, noting (correctly) that such inattention to detail was evidence of a sloppy approach to doing business.

Learn how to get value from dictionaries, usage handbooks, and style guides.

Suggested References:

American Usage and Style: The Consensus
by Roy H. Copperud
(Van Nostrand Reinhold, 1980)

■■

The Associated Press Stylebook and Libel Manual
Revised Edition
(The Associated Press, 1987)

■■

Prentice Hall: Handbook for Writers
(Prentice Hall Inc., 1991)

■■

Webster's Collegiate Dictionary
(latest edition)

NOTE: Buy the latest edition of a reference book whenever you can.

Writing That Gets Results

Most writing has a goal. That goal may be to:

- Win support for a cause;
- Obtain money in next year's scholarships;
- Resolve a customer's complaint or;
- Receive approval for a new program.

Whatever your goal, you're more likely to get results if your, letter, report, or policy is clear, concise and easy to read.

Memos

If possible, use a proven format. Some organizations have style guides that lay out the preferred format. (To, From, Subject, Date, etc.). If you don't have a format to follow, be sure to:

- Address the memo only to the party or parties who must take action on the topic. Too many names create confusion. (You can "cc" others at the bottom.)
- Always include a subject line so your reader knows the topic of the memo up front. If you're responding to someone else's memo, say so in a "Reference" line.
- Write on only one topic. Cramming too many topics into a short memo weakens it and can confuse the reader.
- Clearly state your subject, using simple language.
- Use a positive tone, regardless of what you have to say.
- Use the active voice and personal pronouns.
- Never write anything in a memo that you wouldn't want the entire organization to know.
- Make it a policy that if someone raises a problem, they must also give at least one suggested solution when possible.
- Always end with a call to action. State the response you're looking for (a fax, phone call or meeting) and when you'd like to have it.

Memos are often the quickest, clearest way to communicate.

At Learning Forum, we've found it helpful to leave room for a response on the bottom half of the memo. That way the person reading it can respond right on the form without having to create a new memo. When responding to someone else's memo, I keep a copy for myself. This gives me a record of what was said and reminds me of any action I promised to take.

This method was extremely useful during the time I served as president of the International Alliance for Learning. Because it is an international society, the board members reside all over the world. Regular board meetings happen only once a year, and these busy people sometimes neglected to return calls or respond in writing. When I began my tenure, the previous president told me, "Don't even bother contacting the board. You'll never hear back from them."

My memo system solved that problem. I found that the following elements almost always guaranteed a speedy reply:

- Whenever possible send memos by fax (even better, by e-mail)
- Keep memos short
- Number important items
- Leave room for response, or make boxes for them to check such as Yes, No
- Set a deadline, usually within 24 hours.

Soon I was regularly hearing back from 80 percent of them within 24 hours. (Those who didn't contact me were usually out of town.) If you need to reach a lot of people quickly, give this system a try.

Simplify your life by highlighting incoming memos so that when you sit down to respond, all you need to re-read are the highlighted areas. These sections can also help

Learning Forum's
Memo System

Memo

Date _____

To _____

From _____

Re _____

Problem / Request _____
_____
_____

Suggested Solution _____
_____
_____

Action _____

Respond by _____

To _____

From _____

Reply _____
_____
_____
_____

you organize your memo. And if a quick call will accomplish what a memo would have, only more easily, pick up the phone.

Letters

Your letters say a lot about you as an individual. So, it's important to write the most powerful, productive correspondence you can. Here are some tips:

- Get your reader's attention by identifying your subject up front. Some people actually include a subject line at the top of their letters.

- Create a powerful first paragraph that: lets the reader know what the subject of the letter is; "speaks" in a positive tone; and connects with any previous correspondence or discussion (with reference to a date or subject). This paragraph sets the stage for the whole letter. If it's clear and direct, your reader will carefully read the rest. So make it short (3 or 4 lines), say something concrete, and entice your audience.

- Follow through on promises you made in your opening paragraph. You've got your reader's attention, now keep your promise by writing about the stated subject in a clear, readable style. Include all the information you need to cover in the most organized manner possible. Go back over your brainstorming or clustering list and verify that you've touched on each point. But don't try to cover too many ideas, or you'll lose your audience.

- Forget what you learned in school about paragraphs. Write several short paragraphs instead of one longer one. In fact, it's not uncommon for a letter to be about just one thought. But don't make it one paragraph. Do

Your letters reflect
who you are.

Make them powerful and
productive by:

Getting your reader's attention

∷

Creating a powerful first paragraph

∷

Following through on promises
made in the first paragraph

∷

Writing several short paragraphs instead
of a long one

∷

Asking for what you want

that, and you'll lose your audience for sure.

Instead, break up your writing into more paragraphs, so as to create "white space," making it more visually appealing and therefore easier to read. It's OK to have one-sentence paragraphs.

• Ask for what you want. Think back to when you did your planning. You asked yourself what the purpose of the letter was, and what results you hoped to achieve. Base your request on that . . . and be specific.

Reports

The key to effective report writing is strong organization. The inverted pyramid style of organization on page 23 works well for reports. Start with your conclusions and requests before your discussion and reasons. Put the most important information first and work your way down to the least important. Should your reader choose to not read the entire report, at least you'll have made your most important points.

When you plan a report, take care to target your audience, Mind Map your topic(s), and organize your ideas. The more time you spend preparing up front, the easier the actual writing will be, and the more effectively you'll get your message across.

Now you know the tools and techniques the pros use when they write. You might copy some of the lists in this book and keep them close so you can refer to them when you face a tricky writing task. And remember, no matter how short the document you have to write, always take a few minutes to Plan It. You'll find the job much easier and the result more readable.

When writing reports, put your most important information first.

Should your reader choose to not read the entire report, at least you'll have made your most important points!

Celebrate Your Learning!

! *Is there a way to make the writing process easier?*

Break down the writing process into three steps: Plan It, Write It, and Polish It. A well-organized, clear plan makes writing much easier.

! *Can you learn to write creatively even if your don't consider yourself creative?*

You *are* creative. We all are. You're just letting your overly-critical editor's voice get in your way. Learn to shut down that voice and listen only to your creative writer's voice while you Plan and Write.

! *You're a very good speaker, yet you don't feel as comfortable with your writing. What can you do?*

You've accepted the myth that writing and speaking are two different skills. They're not. When starting a writing project, write just as you would speak. Your writing will become natural and clear.

! *You're unsure of your spelling, and suspect it affects your writing. Is there anything you can do about it?*

Many people have trouble with spelling. It means you have to be diligent about proofreading. There are computer programs available to help you. Make use of these, but always double-check your work.

Since 1981, Learning Forum has produced educational programs for students, educators and business. Its vision is to create a shift in how people learn, so that learning will be joyful, challenging, engaging and meaningful.

Programs and products of Learning Forum—

QUANTUM LEARNING PROGRAMS

Quantum Learning is a comprehensive model of effective learning and teaching. Its programs include: **Quantum Learning for Teachers**, professional development programs for educators providing a proven, research-based approach to the design and delivery of curriculum and the teaching of learning and life skills; **Quantum Learning for Students,** programs that help students master powerful learning and life skills; and **Quantum Learning for Business,** working with companies and organizations to shift training and cultural environments to ones that are both nurturing and effective.

SUPERCAMP

The most innovative and unique program of its kind, SuperCamp incorporates proven, leading edge learning methods that help students succeed through the mastery of academic, social and everyday life skills. Programs are held across the U.S. on prestigious college campuses, as well as internationally, for four age levels: Youth Forum (9-11), Junior Forum (12-13), Senior Forum (14-18), and College Forum (18-24).

SUCCESS PRODUCTS

Learning Forum has brought together a collection of books, video/audio tapes and CD's believed to be the most effective for accelerating growth and learning. The *Quantum Learning Resource Catalog* gives the highlights of best educational methods, along with tips and key points. The Student Success Store focuses on learning and life skills.

For information contact:

LEARNING FORUM
1725 South Coast Highway • Oceanside, CA • 92054-5319 • USA
760.722.0072 • 800.285.3276 • Fax 760.722.3507
email: info@learningforum.com • www.learningforum.com

Great companions to the Quantum Booklet Series are the Learning and Life Skills Videos and CD's

Quantum Reading *The Power to Read Your Best* • Quantum Strategies *Test-Taking – Simply & Effectively* • Winning the Game of School • Increase your Memory Ten Times • How To " Map" Your Way to Better Grades • Be a Confident Math Solver • Take the Mystery Out of Algebra • The Power of Time Management and Goal-Setting • Build a Winning Attitude • Better Friendships • How to Understand and Be Understood • Money: Earning, Saving and Investing It.

Students will excel with valuable skills usable in any subject!

Teachers will get through curriculum faster with deeper meaning and more fun!

Call 800.265.3276 or order online www.learningforumsuccessproducts.com

Bobbi DePorter is president of Learning Forum, producing programs for students, teachers, schools and organizations across the US and internationally. She began her career in real estate development and ventured to co-found a school for entrepreneurs called the Burklyn Business School. She studied with Dr. Georgi Lozanov from Bulgaria, father of accelerated learning, and applied his methods to the school with great results. Having two children and seeing a need to teach students *how to* learn, she then applied the techniques to a program for teenagers called SuperCamp, which has now helped thousands of students relearn how they learn and reshape how they live their lives. In addition to SuperCamp, Learning Forum produces Quantum Learning for Teachers staff development programs for schools, and Quantum Learning for Business for organizations. Bobbi is also a past president of the International Alliance for Learning. She is the author of ten books on the subject of learning. *Quantum Learning: Unleashing the Genius in You, Quantum Teaching: Orchestrating Student Success,* and *Quantum Business: Achieving Success through Quantum Learning* are published in the United States, Great Britain, Germany, Slovenia, Brazil, Russia and Indonesia. These books continue to influence the expansion of Quantum Learning programs and draw international interest.

Mike Hernacki, a former teacher, attorney, and stockbroker, has been a freelance writer and marketing consultant since 1979. He is the author of four books: *The Ultimate Secret to Getting Absolutely Everything You want, The Secret to Conquering Fear, The Forgotten Secret to Phenomenal Success,* and *The Secret to Permanent Prosperity.* His books have been translated into six languages and are sold all over the world. He now divides his time between writing and personal success coaching.